Zoom in on
SUPERHIGHWAYS

Kathy Furgang

Enslow Publishing
101 W. 23rd Street
Suite 240
New York, NY 10011
USA
enslow.com

WORDS TO KNOW

asphalt—Building material used on roadways.

civil engineer—A person who designs and builds structures for a community to use.

concrete—Building material made from a mixture of broken stone, gravel, sand, cement, and water.

earthquake—A natural shaking of the earth's surface.

interstate—A highway that begins and ends in different states.

natural aggregate—Material used under roadways. It is made of sand, gravel, and crushed stone.

suburb—A town that is close to a city.

superhighway—A highway that is made for high-speed travel over long distances.

CONTENTS

The First Highways

How long does it take to get from your home in the city to a friend's home in the country? How long does it take to get from one state to another? What about across the entire United States? It all depends on how you travel. Planes are the fastest way to go long distances, but cars are the most popular way to travel.

For trips less than 250 miles, people usually take a car to get from place to place. That's because the United

States is connected with highways. Thousands of miles of highways connect small towns to big cities. Superhighways allow for high-speed travel over long distances.

Early Roads

Roads have been an important part of the country's growth. In the early days, rough landscape made it hard for horses and carriages to make it over long distances. Roads had to be dug with each new area that people settled.

The first roads were dirt and meant for slow travel.

In the 1750s, George Washington helped build a road through a forest in Ohio. Between 1811 and 1834, the 820-mile National Road replaced it. The strip connected Illinois, Indiana, Maryland, Ohio, Pennsylvania, and West Virginia. This made traveling easier, faster, and safer. The road also allowed people to settle new areas and move supplies.

A Growing Nation

After cars became popular in the early 1900s, there was a need for more roads. There were so many areas to connect!

Miles of Open Road

Today, highways run through both rural and city areas. There are close to 47,000 miles of interstate highways in the United States.

In 1954, President Eisenhower signed a bill to give money to building a better highway system.

It was important that the roadways were smooth for the cars to travel on.

By the 1950s, America was growing fast. President Dwight D. Eisenhower signed the Federal-Aid Highway Act of 1956. This gave money to states to build highways. Missouri, Kansas, and Pennsylvania all got to work right away. They planned and built the first modern interstate highways.

Planning Is Key

There are several stages to making a highway. The first step is to plan it with as much detail as possible. Surveyors are people who measure the exact distances between points of the land. They measure the exact differences in heights of the landscape. This is important when planning roads so they are not too sloped, or slanted.

An engineer looks over plans for a new road. Careful planning is the first step in making superhighways.

When building roads, sometimes nature is affected. Trees may be cut down. Scientists and engineers present designs about what they think should be done. There may be many changes before the plans are approved for construction.

Building Highways

There are many materials used to build highways. After the soil is smoothed and packed down, about 21 inches of natural

Built for Speed

In Germany, there is a highway called the Autobahn. Sections of this 8,047 mile (12,950 km) system of roads have no speed limits at all.

Workers place asphalt as the top layer of a new road.

material is laid down along the entire path. This material, called natural aggregate, is made of sand, gravel, and crushed stone. On top of the aggregate is about 11 inches of concrete and asphalt roadway. This is the part that vehicles ride on.

Some highways may need to pass over waterways. Some pass over other roads, or even underground for short distances. Steel beams are often used to make bridges. The material must be strong enough to hold the load on the bridge.

Tunnels are dug with huge machines. They drill through hard rock. The human-made materials for the tunnel last through all kinds of weather.

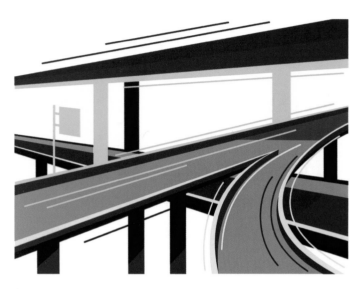

Safety First

One of the most important things about building superhighways is making sure that people travel safely. More than four million people are hurt each year in car accidents. That's why highway safety is so important. Engineers must plan entry and exit ramps carefully. Cars need time to change lanes safely. They must be able to exit the highway without having to slow down too quickly.

Repairing roads is also very important. Concrete and asphalt can expand or contract with the cold and hot weather. That means the material can take up more or less space. These changes can make roads

Sometimes there are accidents on highways. Builders and engineers try to plan roads so they are as safe as possible.

crack and break apart. Repairing them is important so that accidents do not happen.

Protecting Our Roads

Being safe also means making sure roadways can stand up to events such as earthquakes, high winds, or floods. Proper draining systems can help roadways from flooding too quickly. A slightly slanted surface can help rain run to the sides and off the road instead of flooding the roadway.

An Important Job

People who build highways are called civil engineers. A civil engineer plans, designs, and builds projects that are used by the public.

16

Flooding can be dangerous on highways.

Strong but flexible materials can make it harder for roads to be damaged during earthquakes. Bridge materials should be able to twist or bend slightly during an earthquake. This can keep the roadway from breaking or snapping. A road or bridge should be able to stand the load of the cars and the force of the earthquake at the same time.

Cracks can be caused when the roadway temperatures change a lot during the summer and winter.

How Highways Help Us

Great technologies improve people's lives. They may help them do things that were not possible before. They may help them do things faster or easier. Highways have made it possible for cars to reach high speeds safely. Traveling from city to city before cars were invented may have taken days instead of hours. Because of superhighways, people can work farther away from

Highways reduce the amount of time it takes to get places.

home than in the past. Families that live far apart can still visit each other. Superhighways have allowed for the growth of suburbs. Highways connect suburbs all around the country.

Highways have also helped improve car technology. It is important for engineers to make cars that are safe for today's high-speed superhighways. The advances in highways and cars will continue for many years. People spend more time in their cars and on highways today than ever before. They need safe roads and highways that can improve their lives and make travel easy.

Hitting the Road

According to the Federal Highway Administration, the average American drives more than 13,000 miles per year.

ACTIVITY:
TAKE A ROAD TRIP!

Most highways are named with numbers. They run in the direction of east and west or north and south. When we give directions, we name the highway and the direction that a car must move.

Look at the map of North Carolina on page 23. To get from Asheville to Lenoir, take Route 40 east. Then go north on Route 321.

1. Write directions for how to get from Hickory to Charlotte.

2. Write directions for how to get from Greenville to Kitty Hawk.

3. Find a road map of your own (there are many online). Choose a city you would like to visit. Now write out directions from your hometown to that city.

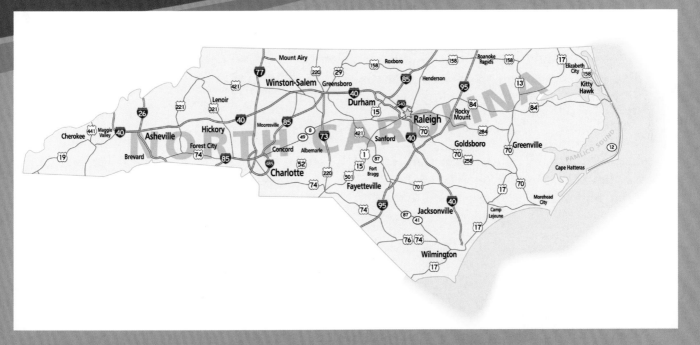

The double blue lines on this map of North Carolina represent major highways, and the red lines show smaller highways.

LEARN MORE

Books

Bethea, Nikole Brooks. *High Tech Highways and Super Skyways: The Next 100 Years of Transportation*. North Mankato, MN: Capstone Press, 2016.

Proudfit, Benjamin. *The Pacific Coast Highway*. New York, NY: Gareth Stevens, 2016.

Proudfit, Benjamin, and Maria Nelson. *The Pan-American Highway*. New York, NY: Gareth Stevens, 2016.

Websites

Federal Highway Administration
www.fhwa.dot.gov/interstate/brainiacs/thingsyoucando.cfm
The article gives ten ideas about how to learn more about the American highway system.

PBS Kids
www.pbs.org/wnet/newyork//laic/episode7/topic3/e7_t3_s3-sh.htm
The article describes the growth of highways as the country expanded to include more suburbs and cities.

INDEX

Published in 2018 by Enslow Publishing, LLC.
101 W. 23rd Street, Suite 240, New York, NY 10011

Library of Congress Cataloging-in-Publication Data
Names: Furgang, Kathy, author.
Title: Zoom in on superhighways / Kathy Furgang.
Description: New York : Enslow Publishing, 2018. | Series: Zoom in on engineering | Includes bibliographical references and index. | Audience: Grade K–3.
Identifiers: LCCN 2017003016| ISBN 9780766087255 (library-bound) | ISBN 9780766088382 (pbk.) | ISBN 9780766088320 (6-pack)
Subjects: LCSH: Roads—Design and construction—Juvenile literature. | Express highways—Juvenile literature. | Express highways—Design and construction—Juvenile literature. | Express highways—Safety measures—Juvenile literature.
Classification: LCC TE149 .F87 2018 | DDC 625.7—dc23
LC record available at https://lccn.loc.gov/2017003016

Printed in the United States of America

To Our Readers: We have done our best to make sure all website addresses in this book were active and appropriate when we went to press. However, the author and the publisher have no control over and assume no liability for the material available on those websites or on any websites they may link to. Any comments or suggestions can be sent by e-mail to customerservice@enslow.com.

Photo Credits: Cover, p. 1 (inset), Sean Pavone/Shutterstock.com; cover, p. 1 (background) ssguy/Shutterstock.com; pp. 2, 3, 22, 23 Vector Tradition/Shutterstock.com; pp. 5, 9, 14, 19 visualgo/DigitalVision Vectors/Getty Images; p. 4 Peter Stuckings/Shutterstock.com; p. 6 Library of Congress/Corbis Historical/Getty Images; p. 8 Corbis Historical/Getty Images; p. 10 BartCo/E+/Getty Images; p. 12 Vadim Ratnikov/Shutterstock.com; p. 15 Glowimages/Getty Images; p. 17 catnap72/E+/Getty Images; p. 18 Steven Puetzer/Photolibrary/Getty Images; p. 20 Michael Melford/The Image Bank; p. 23 Stacey Lynn Payne; graphic elements (Interstate highway sign) Vitezslav Valka/Shutterstock.com.